BIGGEST NAMES IN SPORTS

MATT RYAN

FOOTBALL STAR

by Greg Bates

FOCUS READERS

WWW.FOCUSREADERS.COM

Focus Readers is distributed by North Star Editions:
sales@northstareditions.com | 888-417-0195

Produced for Focus Readers by Red Line Editorial.

Photographs ©: Scott Boehm/AP Images, cover, 1; Ryan Kang/AP Images, 4–5, 6, 9; Seth Poppel/Yearbook Library, 10–11; Michael Dwyer/AP Images, 12, 15; Jason DeCrow/AP Images, 16–17; Brian Garfinkel/AP Images, 18; David Goldman/AP Images, 21; G. Newman Lowrance/AP Images, 22–23; Perry Knotts/AP Images, 25; Curtis Compton/Atlanta Journal-Constitution/AP Images, 27; Red Line Editorial, 29

ISBN
978-1-63517-489-2 (hardcover)
978-1-63517-561-5 (paperback)
978-1-63517-705-3 (ebook pdf)
978-1-63517-633-9 (hosted ebook)

Library of Congress Control Number: 2017948051

Printed in the United States of America
Mankato, MN
November, 2017

ABOUT THE AUTHOR

Greg Bates is a freelance sports journalist based in Green Bay, Wisconsin. He has covered the Green Bay Packers for nearly a decade. He has also written for outlets such as *USA Today Sports Weekly*, the Associated Press, and USA Hockey.

TABLE OF CONTENTS

CHAPTER 1

CHAMPIONSHIP GAME HEROICS

Atlanta Falcons quarterback Matt Ryan took the snap. He dropped back and scanned the field. The Green Bay Packers' defenders knew Ryan had a strong arm. They were ready for a pass. But Ryan saw a hole in the middle of the field. With no defenders nearby, Ryan started running from the Packers' 20-yard line.

Ryan shredded the Packers defense, throwing for 392 yards and four touchdowns.

Ryan sprints toward the end zone for the Falcons' second touchdown of the game.

Ryan faked a throw while on the move. That was enough to freeze a Packers defender. Ryan continued running and dived into the end zone. Falcons fans could hardly believe it. Ryan hadn't run for a touchdown in five years.

Ryan spiked the ball hard, and the hometown crowd roared. The Falcons now had a 17–0 lead. But this wasn't just any game. It was the National Football Conference (NFC) Championship Game after the 2016 season.

Ryan wasn't finished. In the third quarter, the Falcons had the ball on their own 27-yard line. Ryan spotted Julio Jones, one of the best wide receivers in the National Football League (NFL). Ryan threw a laser. Jones caught the pass and raced into the end zone.

Ryan ran down the field to celebrate the 73-yard play. It was his third touchdown pass of the game. And it put the Falcons up 31–0. In the biggest game of his career, Ryan was playing great.

Even with a big lead, the Falcons never let up. Ryan added one more touchdown

MATTY ICE

Every great quarterback has a nickname. Matt Ryan is known as Matty Ice. His high school teammates said he got the name when he was a sophomore. One player claims the nickname stuck because Ryan was always cool under pressure. During games, Ryan can be very calm. Even if his team is losing, Ryan is fearless. He has led several fourth-quarter comebacks.

Ryan waves to the fans after the Falcons' victory in the NFC Championship Game.

pass, for a total of four. The Falcons went on to win the game 44–21. They had earned the right to play in Super Bowl LI.

CHAPTER 2

EARLY DAYS

Matt Ryan was born on May 17, 1985. He grew up in Exton, Pennsylvania, not far from Philadelphia. Even as a kid, Matt was a great athlete. He started playing football when he was only seven years old. He tried a variety of positions. For example, he played tight end, defensive end, and even fullback.

Matt Ryan (2) was the star of his high school football team.

Ryan looks for an open receiver during his sophomore year at Boston College.

Matt was also a pitcher in baseball. When football coaches saw him throw, they moved him to quarterback.

Matt became a three-sport star at William Penn Charter School. He played football, basketball, and baseball. But football was his best sport. He started on the **varsity** team for three years. Many college **scouts** became interested.

Ryan decided to play for Boston College. He didn't see much action as a freshman, though. And the next year, he began the season as the backup quarterback. But the team's starting quarterback struggled. That gave Ryan his opportunity. He started the final four games of the season. He also led his team to a **bowl game**. Ryan threw three touchdown passes in the game to beat Boise State. He was named the game's most valuable player (MVP).

As a junior, Ryan had his best season yet. With his accurate passing, Ryan picked apart defenses. As the full-time starter, he threw for nearly 3,000 yards and had 15 touchdown passes. He also ran for four more scores. Ryan again led his team to a bowl game.

AWARDS ABOUND

Ryan was one of the best players in college football during his senior year. That meant he was nominated for many awards. One major honor was the Heisman Trophy, which is given to the best player in college football. Ryan finished seventh in the voting. The winner that year was Florida quarterback Tim Tebow. However, Ryan was named the Atlantic Coast Conference Player of the Year.

Ryan attempts a pass in a 2006 game against Maryland.

Ryan entered his senior season looking to impress NFL scouts. He did just that. His team won 10 games that season. Ryan threw for more than 4,500 yards. His college career couldn't have been much better. Years after he was done playing, Boston College **retired** his No. 12 jersey.

CHAPTER 3

ROOKIE SENSATION

After college, Matt Ryan entered the 2008 NFL Draft. Most experts considered Ryan the top quarterback in the draft. At the time, the Atlanta Falcons were in search of a new leader. Three quarterbacks played for the team in 2007, and none stood out. The Falcons selected Ryan as the third overall pick.

Ryan shows off his new jersey after being drafted by the Falcons in 2008.

Ryan prepares to take a snap during his rookie season.

Ryan started every game in his **rookie** season. That is rare for a quarterback in his first year in the NFL. And Ryan began with a bang. In the first pass of his career, he threw a touchdown. After the play, he ran down the field to celebrate. Ryan was so excited that he accidentally knocked down one of his teammates.

Ryan played well in his first year. He was named NFL Offensive Rookie of the Year. He even led his team to the **playoffs**.

COMMUNITY SUPPORTER

After settling down in Atlanta, Georgia, Ryan has been a big supporter of the community. He runs the Matt Ryan Foundation. This organization raises money for children's health care. Ryan also helps raise money for Aflac Cancer and Blood Disorders Center. He holds a golf tournament each year, with all the money going toward **charities**.

It was the first time the Falcons had advanced to the postseason in four years.

Ryan's success continued. The Falcons reached the playoffs in four of Ryan's first five seasons. And in the 2012 season, Ryan made it to his first NFC Championship Game. The Falcons hosted the San Francisco 49ers. It was Ryan's first opportunity to make it to the Super Bowl.

In the biggest game of his career, Ryan played great. He threw for nearly 400 yards and had three touchdown passes. The Falcons led 17–0 in the second quarter. Unfortunately for Falcons fans, the 49ers came back and won the

Ryan fires a rocket during the NFC Championship Game against the 49ers.

game. It was a huge disappointment for Ryan. But the loss made him more determined than ever.

CHAPTER 4

SUPER BOWL DISAPPOINTMENT

Matt Ryan made his Super Bowl **debut** in February 2017. The Falcons faced the mighty New England Patriots. Both teams had played great all season. Ryan was hoping to win the first Super Bowl title in Falcons history. Patriots quarterback Tom Brady was trying to win a fifth NFL title for his team.

Ryan heaves a pass in Super Bowl LI.

The Falcons were on fire in the first half. Running back Devonta Freeman ran for a score, and Ryan threw for another. By halftime, the Falcons were up 21–3. Ryan threw another touchdown pass in the third quarter. Leading 28–3, it looked like a Super Bowl victory was within reach.

But the Patriots weren't going to give up. They tied the game late in the fourth quarter on a Brady touchdown pass. For the first time in Super Bowl history, the game went to overtime.

The Falcons didn't get to touch the ball again. On the first drive in overtime, Brady drove the Patriots down the field.

Ryan threw for 284 yards and two touchdowns in Super Bowl LI.

Patriots running back James White finished off the comeback with a 2-yard touchdown run. The Falcons lost the game 34–28. Ryan and his teammates were devastated.

Even though Ryan's team didn't win the Super Bowl, he had an unbelievable season. He was named the league's MVP for 2016. That made him the first Falcons player to win the award. Ryan also won the NFL's Offensive Player of the Year award.

Falcons fans knew they had one of the NFL's best quarterbacks leading their team. They remained hopeful that Ryan would deliver a Super Bowl victory.

Ryan walks off the field after a tough Super Bowl loss.

MATT RYAN

- Height: 6 feet 4 inches (193 cm)
- Weight: 217 pounds (98 kg)
- Birth date: May 17, 1985
- Birthplace: Exton, Pennsylvania
- High school: William Penn Charter School (Philadelphia, Pennsylvania)
- College: Boston College (2004–2007)
- NFL team: Atlanta Falcons (2008–)
- Major awards: NFL Offensive Rookie of the Year (2008); NFL MVP (2016); NFL Offensive Player of the Year (2016)

Boston

Philadelphia

Atlanta

FOCUS ON
MATT RYAN

Write your answers on a separate piece of paper.

1. Write a sentence that describes the main ideas from Chapter 3.

2. When Matt Ryan was in high school, do you think he should have played three sports or concentrated only on football? Why?

3. Which team did Ryan defeat in a college bowl game?

    A. Boston College

    B. Boise State

    C. Florida

4. Why did Boston College retire Ryan's jersey number?

    A. The other players on the team wanted to use the number.

    B. The team thought Ryan's number was bad luck.

    C. Ryan was one of the best players in team history.

Answer key on page 32.

GLOSSARY

bowl game
An extra game at the end of the college football season.

charities
Money or time shared to help others.

debut
First appearance.

playoffs
A set of games played after the regular season to decide which team will be the champion.

retired
When a jersey number may no longer be worn by another player on a team.

rookie
A professional athlete in his or her first year.

scouts
People whose jobs involve looking for talented young players.

varsity
The top team representing a high school or college in a sport or competition.

TO LEARN MORE

BOOKS

Ervin, Phil. *Atlanta Falcons*. Minneapolis: Abdo Publishing, 2016.

Mack, Larry. *The Atlanta Falcons Story*. Minneapolis: Bellwether Media, 2017.

Wyner, Zach. *Atlanta Falcons*. New York: AV2 by Weigl, 2015.

NOTE TO EDUCATORS

Visit **www.focusreaders.com** to find lesson plans, activities, links, and other resources related to this title.

INDEX

Answer Key: **1.** Answers will vary; **2.** Answers will vary; **3.** B; **4.** C